THIS JOURNAL IS CREATED EXCLUSIVELY FOR

_____

FROM

_____

DATE

_____

MY
Conversations
WITH *God*

P.R.A.Y.E.R. JOURNAL

"Write in a book all the words
I have spoken to you."

JEREMIAH 30:2 NIV

My *Conversations* WITH *God*

God longs to have a relationship with you. He wants you to know how much He loves you and that you can experience His love through prayer. Prayer is having a conversation with God, and journaling is a form of prayer. Journaling is a great way to strengthen your faith by sharing your thoughts, feelings, fears, and prayers with God in writing. And through this process, you'll be filled with gratitude and love as you see God's faithfulness in action through His answered prayers.

If you long to be fully known and experience God more intimately, I encourage you to use *My Conversations with God* **P.R.A.Y.E.R.** *Journal* as an expression of prayer to your Heavenly Father. God is so faithful. His promises are true, and when you record your praise, prayers, and petitions to your Heavenly Father, there is transformation in the revelation of His great faithfulness. God is calling you by name, and when you truly listen to what He has to say, He will speak to you because He loves you.

"The gatekeeper opens the gate for him, and the sheep listen to his voice. He calls his own sheep by name and leads them out. When he has brought all his own, he goes on ahead of them, and his sheep follow him because they know his voice."

JOHN 10:3-4 NIV

MY Conversations WITH God

HOW TO USE MY CONVERSATIONS WITH GOD P.R.A.Y.E.R. JOURNAL

There is no right or wrong way to use this journal. The key is to just open yourself up and write whatever is on your heart. Allow the Holy Spirit to speak to you and record what you hear. To assist in this process, I've created a formula to guide you in your journaling as you communicate with God on a daily basis. This formula follows the acronym, P.R.A.Y.E.R.:

P - PRAISE

R - REPENT

A - ASK

Y - YIELD

E - ENTER

R - RESPOND

My prayer for you, is that *My Conversations with God P.R.A.Y.E.R. Journal* will strengthen and deepen your relationship with God. Through your journal writing, I pray that you see the wonder and awesome power of Almighty God at work in your life. He loves you. He's faithful to you, and, He wants to have a relationship with you.

Michelle Prince

P – PRAISE

Thank God for all His wonderful deeds. Thank him for His goodness, His power, His mercy, His wisdom, and love. Write out your praises to God and give glory to your Father who is faithful to you!

"I will give thanks to you, Lord, with all my heart; I will tell of all your wonderful deeds. I will be glad and rejoice in you; I will sing the praises of your name, O Most High." PSALM 9:1-2 NIV

R – REPENT

Recognize and repent for your sins. Let God know, through your journal writing, about the areas of your life where you have fallen short and are in need of forgiveness. God already knows your sins, but it's in the act of repentance that we are in agreement with God, which will honor and create a closer, more intimate relationship with Him.

"If we claim to be without sin, we deceive ourselves and the truth is not in us. If we confess our sins, he is faithful and just and will forgive us our sins and purify us from all unrighteousness." 1 JOHN 1:8-9 NIV

A – ASK

Ask God for the things you desire. God is a good and loving Father who takes delight in His children. He wants to give us the desires of our heart, but first we must ask. Write out and ask God for what you want and need, but also know that God will only give you what He believes is best for you.

"Ask and it will be given to you, seek and you will find; knock and the door will be opened for you. For everyone who asks receives; the one who seeks finds; and the one who knocks, the door will be opened." MATTHEW 7:7-8 NIV

Y – YIELD

To yield means to listen. After you have given praise to God for his goodness, repented for your sins, and asked for His help, now is the time to be quiet and just listen. God speaks to us and when you regularly take time to listen, you will hear His voice.

"Call to me and I will answer you and tell you great and unsearchable things you do not know." JEREMIAH 33:3 NIV

E – ENTER

Now that you've heard God speak to you, enter it in your journal. Write it down. It's amazing the revelation that God will reveal to us when we take the time to listen. It's equally important that we don't just hear His voice, but that we record it, too. Keeping a record of what God has said to you is a great way to build your relationship with God. When you are able to go back and see how faithful God has been to you, you will be grateful and strengthened in your faith.

"This is what the Lord, the God of Israel, says: Write in a book all the words I have spoken to you." JEREMIAH 30:2 NIV

R – RESPOND

Whatever God is telling you to do, it's time to respond … to obey. If you obey the Lord's commands, He will give you the courage, strength, and grace to complete any task. And in doing so, your obedience will be a sincere act of worship to Him. So once you've received your marching orders from God, it's best to not delay in your obedience. Doing so can lead to sin and muffle the voice of God from giving you any more direction.

"Anyone who loves me will obey my teaching. My Father will love them, and we will come to them and make our home with them." JOHN 14:23 NIV

DATE _____

P — PRAISE - God you are so good to me! Thank you for your love, protection, and faithfulness to me and my family. Thank you for healing Mom's sickness and for giving her a full recovery!

R — REPENT - Please forgive me for my selfishness and how I handled the situation with Carol last night. I know my words did not honor you or make her feel good, so please forgive me.

A — ASK - Please help me to love others more, especially when we disagree. Please bless my children and keep them safe. Please show me how I can better serve you.

Y — YIELD - Lord, I'll stop now and turn my attention to you. I'm ready to listen ...please speak to me.

E — ENTER - I heard in my spirit that I should apologize to Carol for how I reacted. I also felt that you want me to spend more time with you by reading your Word.

R — RESPOND - Lord, I will obey what I heard and call Carol as soon as I finish journaling. I will set aside an extra 20 minutes tomorrow morning to read your Word and spend time with you in prayer before I start my day.

Ask AND IT WILL BE *given to you;*
SEEK AND YOU WILL FIND; *knock and*
the door WILL BE OPENED TO YOU.

MATTHEW 7:7

Use this space to write whatever is on your heart

DATE _____

P – PRAISE

R – REPENT

A – ASK

Y – YIELD

E – ENTER

R – RESPOND

MY CONVERSATIONS WITH GOD

Ask AND IT WILL BE *given to you;*
SEEK AND YOU WILL FIND; *knock and*
the door WILL BE OPENED TO YOU.
MATTHEW 7:7

DATE _____

P – PRAISE

R – REPENT

A – ASK

Y – YIELD

E – ENTER

R – RESPOND

MY CONVERSATIONS WITH GOD

Put on THE FULL ARMOR OF GOD,
SO THAT YOU CAN *take your stand*
AGAINST THE DEVIL'S SCHEMES.
EPHESIANS 6:11

DATE _____

P – PRAISE
_____
_____

R – REPENT
_____
_____

A – ASK
_____
_____

Y – YIELD
_____
_____

E – ENTER
_____
_____

R – RESPOND
_____
_____

MY CONVERSATIONS WITH GOD

FOR I KNOW THE *plans I have* FOR YOU,
DECLARES THE LORD, PLANS TO *prosper you* AND NOT TO
HARM YOU, PLANS TO *give you hope* AND A FUTURE.
JEREMIAH 29:11

DATE _____

P – PRAISE

R – REPENT

A – ASK

Y – YIELD

E – ENTER

R – RESPOND

MY CONVERSATIONS WITH GOD

BUT, SEEK FIRST *his* KINGDOM AND HIS
RIGHTEOUSNESS, AND ALL THESE
THINGS WILL BE *given to you* AS WELL.
MATTHEW 6:33

_____

_____

_____

_____

_____

_____

_____

_____

_____

_____

_____

_____

_____

_____

_____

DATE _____

P – PRAISE
_____
_____

R – REPENT
_____
_____

A – ASK
_____
_____

Y – YIELD
_____
_____

E – ENTER
_____
_____

R – RESPOND
_____
_____
_____

MY CONVERSATIONS WITH GOD

DATE _____

P – PRAISE
_____
_____

R – REPENT
_____
_____

A – ASK
_____
_____

Y – YIELD
_____
_____

E – ENTER
_____
_____

R – RESPOND
_____
_____
_____

MY CONVERSATIONS WITH GOD

BLESSED IS THE ONE *who trusts*
IN THE LORD, WHOSE
CONFIDENCE IS IN *him*.
JEREMIAH 17:7

DATE _____

P – PRAISE

R – REPENT

A – ASK

Y – YIELD

E – ENTER

R – RESPOND

MY CONVERSATIONS WITH GOD

P – PRAISE
_____
_____

R – REPENT
_____
_____

A – ASK
_____
_____

Y – YIELD
_____
_____

E – ENTER
_____
_____

R – RESPOND
_____
_____
_____

MY CONVERSATIONS WITH GOD

For I am THE LORD YOUR GOD who takes hold OF YOUR RIGHT HAND, AND SAYS TO YOU, DO NOT FEAR; I WILL help you.

ISAIAH 41:13

DATE _____

P – PRAISE
_____
_____

R – REPENT
_____
_____

A – ASK
_____
_____

Y – YIELD
_____
_____

E – ENTER
_____
_____

R – RESPOND
_____
_____
_____

AND GOD IS *able to* BLESS YOU ABUNDANTLY, SO
THAT IN ALL THINGS AT *all times*, HAVING ALL THAT
you need, YOU WILL ABOUND IN EVERY *good work*.
2 CORINTHIANS 9:8

P – PRAISE

R – REPENT

A – ASK

Y – YIELD

E – ENTER

R – RESPOND

MY CONVERSATIONS WITH GOD

I AM WITH YOU AND WILL WATCH OVER YOU WHEREVER YOU GO, AND I WILL *bring you back* TO THIS LAND. I WILL NOT *leave you until* I HAVE DONE WHAT I HAVE *promised you.*

GENESIS 28:15

DATE _____

P – PRAISE

R – REPENT

A – ASK

Y – YIELD

E – ENTER

R – RESPOND

MY CONVERSATIONS WITH GOD

REJOICE ALWAYS, PRAY CONTINUALLY, GIVE
thanks in all CIRCUMSTANCES; FOR THIS IS
God's will FOR YOU IN *Christ Jesus.*
1 THESSALONIANS 5:16-18

DATE _____

P — PRAISE

R — REPENT

A — ASK

Y — YIELD

E — ENTER

R — RESPOND

MY CONVERSATIONS WITH GOD

So IN EVERYTHING, DO TO OTHERS WHAT
YOU WOULD HAVE THEM *do to you*, FOR THIS
sums up THE LAW AND THE PROPHETS.

2 CORINTHIANS 9:8

DATE _____

P – PRAISE
_____
_____

R – REPENT
_____
_____

A – ASK
_____
_____

Y – YIELD
_____
_____

E – ENTER
_____
_____

R – RESPOND
_____
_____

MY CONVERSATIONS WITH GOD

Honor YOUR FATHER AND YOUR MOTHER,
SO THAT YOU MAY *live long* IN THE LAND
THE LORD YOUR *God is giving* YOU.
EXODUS 20:12

DATE _____

P – PRAISE

R – REPENT

A – ASK

Y – YIELD

E – ENTER

R – RESPOND

MY CONVERSATIONS WITH GOD

HE GIVES STRENGTH
to the weary AND INCREASES
the power OF THE WEAK.
ISAIAH 40:29

P – PRAISE

_____

_____

R – REPENT

_____

_____

A – ASK

_____

_____

Y – YIELD

_____

_____

E – ENTER

_____

_____

R – RESPOND

_____

_____

MY CONVERSATIONS WITH GOD

IF YOU LACK WISDOM, YOU SHOULD ASK GOD,
WHO *gives* GENEROUSLY TO *all without*
FINDING FAULT, AND IT WILL BE *given to you.*
JAMES 1:5

DATE _____

P – PRAISE

R – REPENT

A – ASK

Y – YIELD

E – ENTER

R – RESPOND

MY CONVERSATIONS WITH GOD

Submit YOURSELVES, THEN,
to God. RESIST THE DEVIL,
AND HE WILL *flee* FROM YOU.
JAMES 4:7

DATE _____

P – PRAISE
_____
_____

R – REPENT
_____
_____

A – ASK
_____

Y – YIELD
_____

E – ENTER
_____
_____

R – RESPOND
_____
_____

MY CONVERSATIONS WITH GOD

The Lord HIMSELF GOES BEFORE YOU, AND WILL
be with YOU; HE WILL NEVER LEAVE YOU NOR FORSAKE YOU.
Do not BE AFRAID; DO NOT BE DISCOURAGED.

DEUTERONOMY 31:8

DATE _____

P – PRAISE
_____
_____

R – REPENT
_____
_____

A – ASK
_____
_____

Y – YIELD
_____
_____

E – ENTER
_____
_____

R – RESPOND
_____
_____
_____

MY CONVERSATIONS WITH GOD

FOR GOD SO *loved the world* THAT HE GAVE
HIS ONE AND *only* SON, THAT WHOEVER *believes*
IN HIM SHALL NOT PERISH BUT *have* ETERNAL LIFE.

JOHN 3:16

DATE _____

P – PRAISE
_____
_____

R – REPENT
_____
_____

A – ASK
_____
_____

Y – YIELD
_____
_____

E – ENTER
_____
_____

R – RESPOND
_____
_____
_____

MY CONVERSATIONS WITH GOD

THEREFORE I TELL YOU, WHATEVER
YOU ASK FOR *in prayer*, BELIEVE *that* YOU
HAVE *received it*, AND IT WILL BE YOURS.

MARK 11:24

DATE _____

P – PRAISE

_____

_____

R – REPENT

_____

_____

A – ASK

_____

_____

Y – YIELD

_____

_____

E – ENTER

_____

_____

R – RESPOND

_____

_____

_____

MY CONVERSATIONS WITH GOD

BUT THOSE WHO *hope* IN THE LORD WILL RENEW THEIR STRENGTH.
THEY WILL *soar on wings* LIKE EAGLES; THEY WILL *run* AND NOT
GROW WEARY, THEY WILL *walk* AND NOT BE FAINT.

ISAIAH 40:31

DATE _____

P – PRAISE

_____

_____

R – REPENT

_____

_____

A – ASK

_____

_____

Y – YIELD

_____

_____

E – ENTER

_____

_____

R – RESPOND

_____

_____

_____

MY CONVERSATIONS WITH GOD

SO IF THE SON SETS YOU *free*,
YOU WILL BE *free* INDEED.
JOHN 8:36

DATE _____

P – PRAISE

R – REPENT

A – ASK

Y – YIELD

E – ENTER

R – RESPOND

MY CONVERSATIONS WITH GOD

HAVE I NOT COMMANDED YOU? BE *strong* AND COURAGEOUS. DO NOT *be afraid*; DO NOT BE DISCOURAGED, FOR THE LORD YOUR GOD WILL BE *with you* WHEREVER YOU GO.

JOSHUA 1:9

P – PRAISE

_____

_____

R – REPENT

_____

_____

A – ASK

_____

_____

Y – YIELD

_____

_____

E – ENTER

_____

_____

R – RESPOND

_____

_____

_____

MY CONVERSATIONS WITH GOD

AND MY GOD WILL MEET ALL
your needs ACCORDING TO THE
riches OF HIS *glory* IN CHRIST JESUS.
PHILIPPIANS 4:19

P — PRAISE

R — REPENT

A — ASK

Y — YIELD

E — ENTER

R — RESPOND

Though THE MOUNTAINS BE SHAKEN AND THE HILLS
BE REMOVED, YET MY UNFAILING *love for you,*
will not be shaken NOR MY COVENANT OF *peace* BE
REMOVED, SAYS THE LORD, WHO *has compassion* ON YOU.

ISAIAH 54:10

P – PRAISE

R – REPENT

A – ASK

Y – YIELD

E – ENTER

R – RESPOND

THE RIGHTEOUS CRY OUT, AND THE
Lord hears THEM; HE *delivers*
THEM FROM *all* THEIR TROUBLES.
PSALM 34:17

P – PRAISE

R – REPENT

A – ASK

Y – YIELD

E – ENTER

R – RESPOND

CALL ON ME IN THE DAY
OF TROUBLE; I WILL *deliver*
you, AND YOU WILL *honor* ME.
PSALM 50:15

DATE _____

P – PRAISE
_____
_____

R – REPENT
_____
_____

A – ASK
_____
_____

Y – YIELD
_____
_____

E – ENTER
_____
_____

R – RESPOND
_____
_____

MY CONVERSATIONS WITH GOD

AND WE KNOW THAT IN *all things* GOD WORKS
FOR *the good* OF THOSE WHO LOVE HIM, WHO
HAVE BEEN CALLED ACCORDING TO *his purpose.*
ROMANS 8:28

DATE _____

P – PRAISE

_____

_____

R – REPENT

_____

_____

A – ASK

_____

_____

Y – YIELD

_____

_____

E – ENTER

_____

_____

R – RESPOND

_____

_____

_____

MY CONVERSATIONS WITH GOD

IF YOU DECLARE WITH YOUR MOUTH, *"Jesus is Lord,"* AND BELIEVE IN YOUR *heart* THAT GOD *raised him* FROM THE DEAD, YOU *will be saved.* FOR IT IS WITH YOUR HEART THAT YOU *believe* AND ARE JUSTIFIED, AND IT IS *with your mouth that you* PROFESS YOUR FAITH AND ARE *saved.*

ROMANS 10:9–10

_____

_____

_____

_____

_____

_____

_____

_____

_____

_____

_____

_____

_____

_____

_____

_____

_____

_____

_____

DATE _____

P – PRAISE

R – REPENT

A – ASK

Y – YIELD

E – ENTER

R – RESPOND

MY CONVERSATIONS WITH GOD

THE LORD IS CLOSE TO THE
BROKENHEARTED AND *saves* THOSE
WHO ARE *crushed in spirit.*
PSALM 34:18

DATE _____

P – PRAISE
_____

_____

R – REPENT
_____

_____

A – ASK
_____

_____

Y – YIELD
_____

_____

E – ENTER
_____

_____

R – RESPOND
_____

_____

_____

MY CONVERSATIONS WITH GOD

Do not be anxious ABOUT ANYTHING, BUT IN EVERY SITUATION, BY *prayer* AND PETITION, WITH THANKSGIVING, *present your requests* TO GOD. AND THE *peace of God*, WHICH TRANSCENDS ALL UNDERSTANDING, WILL GUARD YOUR HEARTS AND YOUR *mind in Christ Jesus*.

PHILIPPIANS 4:6–7

DATE _____

P – PRAISE
_____
_____

R – REPENT
_____
_____

A – ASK
_____
_____

Y – YIELD
_____
_____

E – ENTER
_____
_____

R – RESPOND
_____
_____

MY CONVERSATIONS WITH GOD

Trust in the Lord WITH ALL YOUR HEART, AND LEAN NOT ON YOUR *own* UNDERSTANDING; IN ALL YOUR WAYS *submit to him*, AND HE WILL MAKE *your paths straight.*

PROVERBS 3:5–6

DATE _____

P – PRAISE
_____
_____

R – REPENT
_____
_____

A – ASK
_____
_____

Y – YIELD
_____
_____

E – ENTER
_____
_____

R – RESPOND
_____
_____

MY CONVERSATIONS WITH GOD

Come to me, ALL WHO ARE WEARY AND BURDENED, AND I will give you rest.
MATTHEW 11:28

DATE _____

P – PRAISE

R – REPENT

A – ASK

Y – YIELD

E – ENTER

R – RESPOND

MY CONVERSATIONS WITH GOD

TAKE DELIGHT IN THE LORD,
AND HE WILL *give* YOU THE
desires of your heart.
PSALM 37:4

DATE _____

P – PRAISE

R – REPENT

A – ASK

Y – YIELD

E – ENTER

R – RESPOND

MY CONVERSATIONS WITH GOD

AND I *will do* WHATEVER YOU ASK IN
MY NAME, SO THAT THE FATHER
may be GLORIFIED IN THE SON.
JOHN 14:13

DATE _____

P – PRAISE

R – REPENT

A – ASK

Y – YIELD

E – ENTER

R – RESPOND

MY CONVERSATIONS WITH GOD

AND I PRAY THAT YOU, BEING ROOTED AND
established in love, MAY HAVE POWER, TOGETHER
WITH ALL THE LORD'S HOLY PEOPLE, TO *grasp how wide*
AND *long and high* AND DEEP IS THE *love of Christ.*

EPHESIANS 3:17–18

_____

_____

_____

_____

_____

_____

_____

_____

_____

_____

_____

_____

_____

_____

_____

_____

_____

_____

DATE _____

P – PRAISE

_____

_____

R – REPENT

_____

_____

A – ASK

_____

_____

Y – YIELD

_____

_____

E – ENTER

_____

_____

R – RESPOND

_____

_____

_____

MY CONVERSATIONS WITH GOD

BECAUSE OF THE LORD'S *great love we* ARE NOT CONSUMED, FOR HIS COMPASSIONS *never fail.* THEY ARE *new* EVERY MORNING; *great* IS YOUR FAITHFULNESS.
LAMENTATIONS 3:22-23

DATE _____

P – PRAISE

R – REPENT

A – ASK

Y – YIELD

E – ENTER

R – RESPOND

MY CONVERSATIONS WITH GOD

THERE IS A *time* FOR EVERYTHING,
AND A SEASON FOR *every*
activity UNDER THE HEAVENS.
ECCLESIASTES 3:1

P – PRAISE

R – REPENT

A – ASK

Y – YIELD

E – ENTER

R – RESPOND

WHEN YOU PASS THROUGH THE WATERS, I *will* BE WITH YOU;
AND WHEN YOU *pass through the rivers*, THEY WILL NOT SWEEP
OVER YOU. WHEN YOU *walk* THROUGH THE FIRE, YOU WILL
NOT BE BURNED; THE FLAMES *will not* SET YOU ABLAZE.

ISAIAH 43:2

DATE _____

P – PRAISE

R – REPENT

A – ASK

Y – YIELD

E – ENTER

R – RESPOND

MY CONVERSATIONS WITH GOD

The END OF THE MATTER IS *better*
THAN THE BEGINNING, AND
PATIENCE IS *better than pride.*
ECCLESIASTES 7:8

DATE _____

P – PRAISE

R – REPENT

A – ASK

Y – YIELD

E – ENTER

R – RESPOND

MY CONVERSATIONS WITH GOD

THEREFORE, THERE IS NOW NO
CONDEMNATION FOR *those*
WHO ARE *in Christ Jesus.*
ROMANS 8:1

DATE _____

P – PRAISE
_____
_____

R – REPENT
_____
_____

A – ASK
_____
_____

Y – YIELD
_____
_____

E – ENTER
_____
_____

R – RESPOND
_____
_____
_____

MY CONVERSATIONS WITH GOD

For he WILL COMMAND his
ANGELS CONCERNING YOU, to guard
YOU IN ALL YOUR WAYS.
PSALM 91:11

DATE _____

P – PRAISE

R – REPENT

A – ASK

Y – YIELD

E – ENTER

R – RESPOND

MY CONVERSATIONS WITH GOD

For the spirit GOD GAVE US DOES NOT MAKE US TIMID, BUT GIVES US *power*, LOVE AND SELF-DISCIPLINE.

2 TIMOTHY 1:7

P – PRAISE

R – REPENT

A – ASK

Y – YIELD

E – ENTER

R – RESPOND

IN YOUR ANGER DO *not sin:*
DO NOT LET THE SUN GO DOWN
WHILE YOU *are still angry.*
EPHESIANS 4:26

P – PRAISE

R – REPENT

A – ASK

Y – YIELD

E – ENTER

R – RESPOND

MY CONVERSATIONS WITH GOD

HE HAS *shown you what* IS GOOD. AND WHAT DOES
THE LORD REQUIRE OF YOU? TO ACT JUSTLY AND TO LOVE
mercy and to WALK HUMBLY WITH YOUR *God.*
JEREMIAH 33:3

DATE _____

P – PRAISE

R – REPENT

A – ASK

Y – YIELD

E – ENTER

R – RESPOND

MY CONVERSATIONS WITH GOD

Call TO ME AND I WILL ANSWER YOU,
AND TELL YOU *great* AND UNSEARCHABLE
things YOU DO NOT KNOW.
MICAH 6:8

_____
_____
_____
_____
_____
_____
_____
_____
_____
_____
_____
_____
_____
_____
_____
_____
_____
_____
_____
_____

DATE _____

P – PRAISE

R – REPENT

A – ASK

Y – YIELD

E – ENTER

R – RESPOND

MY CONVERSATIONS WITH GOD

AND SURELY I AM WITH *you*,
ALWAYS TO THE
very end of the age.
MATTHEW 28:20

P – PRAISE

_____

_____

R – REPENT

_____

_____

A – ASK

_____

_____

Y – YIELD

_____

_____

E – ENTER

_____

_____

R – RESPOND

_____

_____

MY CONVERSATIONS WITH GOD

Bring the whole tithe INTO THE STOREHOUSE, THAT THERE MAY BE FOOD IN MY *house*. *Test me* IN THIS, SAYS THE LORD *Almighty*, AND SEE IF I WILL NOT THROW OPEN THE FLOODGATES OF HEAVEN AND *pour out* SO MUCH *blessing* THAT THERE WILL NOT BE ROOM ENOUGH *to store it*.

MALACHI 3:10

DATE _____

P – PRAISE

R – REPENT

A – ASK

Y – YIELD

E – ENTER

R – RESPOND

MY CONVERSATIONS WITH GOD

SO DO NOT FEAR, FOR I AM *with you*; DO NOT BE DISMAYED,
FOR I AM YOUR GOD. *I will* STRENGTHEN YOU AND
help you; I WILL UPHOLD YOU WITH MY *righteous right hand.*

ISAIAH 41:10

DATE _____

P – PRAISE

R – REPENT

A – ASK

Y – YIELD

E – ENTER

R – RESPOND

MY CONVERSATIONS WITH GOD

P – PRAISE

_____

_____

R – REPENT

_____

_____

A – ASK

_____

_____

Y – YIELD

_____

_____

E – ENTER

_____

_____

R – RESPOND

_____

_____

_____

YOU ARE THE *light of the world*. A TOWN *built* ON A HILL CANNOT BE HIDDEN. NEITHER DO PEOPLE LIGHT A LAMP AND PUT IT UNDER A *bowl*. INSTEAD THEY PUT IT ON ITS STAND, AND IT GIVES LIGHT TO *everyone in the house*. IN THE SAME WAY, LET YOUR LIGHT *shine* BEFORE OTHERS, THAT THEY MAY SEE YOUR GOOD DEEDS AND *glorify your Father* IN HEAVEN.

MATTHEW 5:14-16

DATE _____

P – PRAISE

R – REPENT

A – ASK

Y – YIELD

E – ENTER

R – RESPOND

MY CONVERSATIONS WITH GOD

Wait FOR THE LORD,
be strong AND TAKE HEART
AND WAIT FOR THE *Lord*.
PSALM 27:14

DATE _____

P – PRAISE

R – REPENT

A – ASK

Y – YIELD

E – ENTER

R – RESPOND

MY CONVERSATIONS WITH GOD

Do not let ANY UNWHOLESOME *talk come out* OF YOUR MOUTH, BUT ONLY WHAT IS HELPFUL FOR *building* OTHERS UP ACCORDING TO THEIR NEEDS, THAT IT MAY *benefit those who listen.*

EPHESIANS 4:29

P – PRAISE

R – REPENT

A – ASK

Y – YIELD

E – ENTER

R – RESPOND

I HAVE TOLD YOU THESE THINGS,
SO THAT IN ME YOU *may have peace.*
IN THIS WORLD YOU WILL HAVE TROUBLE.
But take heart! I HAVE OVERCOME *the world.*
JOHN 16:33

DATE _____

P – PRAISE

_____

_____

R – REPENT

_____

_____

A – ASK

_____

_____

Y – YIELD

_____

_____

E – ENTER

_____

_____

R – RESPOND

_____

_____

MY CONVERSATIONS WITH GOD

See WHAT GREAT LOVE THE *Father has* LAVISHED
ON US, THAT WE SHOULD BE *called* CHILDREN
OF GOD! AND THAT IS WHAT WE ARE! THE REASON THE
world DOES NOT *know us* IS THAT IT DID NOT *know him.*

1 JOHN 3:1

DATE _____

P – PRAISE

_____

_____

R – REPENT

_____

_____

A – ASK

_____

_____

Y – YIELD

_____

_____

E – ENTER

_____

_____

R – RESPOND

_____

_____

MY CONVERSATIONS WITH GOD

LET US NOT *become weary* IN DOING GOOD,
FOR AT THE *proper time* WE WILL
reap a harvest IF WE DO NOT *give* UP.
GALATIANS 6:9

DATE _____

P – PRAISE
_____
_____

R – REPENT
_____
_____

A – ASK
_____
_____

Y – YIELD
_____
_____

E – ENTER
_____
_____

R – RESPOND
_____
_____
_____

MY CONVERSATIONS WITH GOD

So *whether* YOU EAT OR DRINK
OR WHATEVER *you do,*
DO IT ALL FOR THE *glory of God.*
1 CORINTHIANS 10:31

DATE _____

P – PRAISE

R – REPENT

A – ASK

Y – YIELD

E – ENTER

R – RESPOND

MY CONVERSATIONS WITH GOD

LOVE THE LORD YOUR GOD WITH *all your heart*
AND WITH ALL YOUR *soul* AND WITH *all your strength* AND
WITH ALL YOUR MIND; AND, *love your neighbor* AS YOURSELF.

LUKE 10:27

DATE _____

P – PRAISE

R – REPENT

A – ASK

Y – YIELD

E – ENTER

R – RESPOND

MY CONVERSATIONS WITH GOD

The Sovereign LORD WILL WIPE AWAY THE *tears* FROM ALL FACES; HE WILL REMOVE HIS PEOPLE'S DISGRACE FROM *all the earth.*

ISAIAH 25:8

DATE _____

P – PRAISE

_____

_____

R – REPENT

_____

_____

A – ASK

_____

_____

Y – YIELD

_____

_____

E – ENTER

_____

_____

R – RESPOND

_____

_____

MY CONVERSATIONS WITH GOD

BUT *seek first his* KINGDOM AND HIS
RIGHTEOUSNESS, AND ALL THESE
THINGS WILL BE *given to you* AS WELL.
MATTHEW 6:33

DATE _____

P – PRAISE

_____

_____

R – REPENT

_____

_____

A – ASK

_____

_____

Y – YIELD

_____

_____

E – ENTER

_____

_____

R – RESPOND

_____

_____

MY CONVERSATIONS WITH GOD

A CHEERFUL HEART IS *good*
medicine BUT A CRUSHED SPIRIT
DRIES UP THE *bones.*
PROVERBS 17:22

DATE _____

P – PRAISE

R – REPENT

A – ASK

Y – YIELD

E – ENTER

R – RESPOND

MY CONVERSATIONS WITH GOD

BLESSED ARE THOSE WHO *hunger*
and thirst FOR RIGHTEOUSNESS,
FOR THEY *will be filled.*
MATTHEW 5:6

DATE _____

P – PRAISE

_____
_____

R – REPENT

_____
_____

A – ASK

_____
_____

Y – YIELD

_____
_____

E – ENTER

_____
_____

R – RESPOND

_____
_____

MY CONVERSATIONS WITH GOD

DATE _____

P – PRAISE

_____

_____

R – REPENT

_____

_____

A – ASK

_____

_____

Y – YIELD

_____

_____

E – ENTER

_____

_____

R – RESPOND

_____

_____

_____

MY CONVERSATIONS WITH GOD

Be kind AND COMPASSIONATE TO
ONE ANOTHER, FORGIVING *each other,*
JUST AS IN *Christ* GOD FORGAVE YOU.

EPHESIANS 4:32

DATE _____

P – PRAISE
_____
_____

R – REPENT
_____
_____

A – ASK
_____
_____

Y – YIELD
_____
_____

E – ENTER
_____
_____

R – RESPOND
_____
_____
_____

MY CONVERSATIONS WITH GOD

DO NOTHING OUT OF SELFISH AMBITION OR VAIN CONCEIT. *Rather*, IN HUMILITY *value others* ABOVE YOURSELVES.

PHILIPPIANS 2:3

DATE _____

P – PRAISE

_____

_____

R – REPENT

_____

_____

A – ASK

_____

_____

Y – YIELD

_____

_____

E – ENTER

_____

_____

R – RESPOND

_____

_____

MY CONVERSATIONS WITH GOD

TAKE MY *yoke upon you* AND LEARN FROM *me*,
FOR I AM GENTLE AND *humble in heart*,
AND YOU WILL *find rest* FOR YOUR SOULS.
MATTHEW 11:29

DATE _____

P – PRAISE
_____
_____

R – REPENT
_____
_____

A – ASK
_____
_____

Y – YIELD
_____
_____

E – ENTER
_____
_____

R – RESPOND
_____
_____
_____

MY CONVERSATIONS WITH GOD

DATE _____

P — PRAISE
_____
_____

R — REPENT
_____
_____

A — ASK
_____
_____

Y — YIELD
_____
_____

E — ENTER
_____
_____

R — RESPOND
_____
_____

MY CONVERSATIONS WITH GOD

DO NOT *conform* TO THE PATTERN OF THIS WORLD,
BUT BE TRANSFORMED BY THE *renewing* OF YOUR MIND.
THEN YOU WILL BE *able* TO TEST AND APPROVE WHAT
GOD'S WILL IS – HIS GOOD, PLEASING AND *perfect* WILL.

ROMANS 12:2

P – PRAISE

R – REPENT

A – ASK

Y – YIELD

E – ENTER

R – RESPOND

THIS IS THE CONFIDENCE WE HAVE IN APPROACHING
God: THAT IF WE ASK *anything according*
TO HIS WILL, HE *hears* US.

1 JOHN 5:14

DATE _____

P – PRAISE

R – REPENT

A – ASK

Y – YIELD

E – ENTER

R – RESPOND

MY CONVERSATIONS WITH GOD

THEREFORE, *as God's chosen* PEOPLE, HOLY AND
DEARLY LOVED, CLOTHE YOURSELVES WITH *compassion,*
kindness, HUMILITY, GENTLENESS AND PATIENCE.
COLOSSIANS 3:13

DATE _____

P – PRAISE

R – REPENT

A – ASK

Y – YIELD

E – ENTER

R – RESPOND

MY CONVERSATIONS WITH GOD

FOR THE LORD *your God* IS *the one who goes* WITH YOU TO FIGHT FOR YOU AGAINST YOUR ENEMIES TO *give you victory.*

DEUTERONOMY 20:4

DATE _____

P – PRAISE

R – REPENT

A – ASK

Y – YIELD

E – ENTER

R – RESPOND

MY CONVERSATIONS WITH GOD

NEITHER HEIGHT NOR DEPTH, NO ANYTHING
ELSE IN *all creation* WILL BE ABLE TO SEPARATE YOU,
FROM THE *love of God* THAT IS IN CHRIST JESUS *our Lord.*
ROMANS 8:39

DATE _____

P – PRAISE

R – REPENT

A – ASK

Y – YIELD

E – ENTER

R – RESPOND

MY CONVERSATIONS WITH GOD

DATE _____

P – PRAISE
_____
_____

R – REPENT
_____
_____

A – ASK
_____
_____

Y – YIELD
_____
_____

E – ENTER
_____
_____

R – RESPOND
_____
_____
_____

MY CONVERSATIONS WITH GOD

NO WEAPON FORGED AGAINST
YOU *will prevail*, AND YOU WILL REFUTE
EVERY TONGUE THAT ACCUSES YOU.
ISAIAH 54:17

DATE _____

P – PRAISE

R – REPENT

A – ASK

Y – YIELD

E – ENTER

R – RESPOND

MY CONVERSATIONS WITH GOD

But the Lord is faithful, AND HE
WILL STRENGTHEN YOU, AND
PROTECT YOU FROM THE EVIL ONE.
2 THESSALONIANS 3:3

P – PRAISE

_____

_____

R – REPENT

_____

_____

A – ASK

_____

_____

Y – YIELD

_____

_____

E – ENTER

_____

_____

R – RESPOND

_____

_____

_____

MY CONVERSATIONS WITH GOD

PEACE I LEAVE WITH YOU; *my peace I give you.*
I DO NOT GIVE TO YOU AS THE WORLD GIVES. DO NOT LET
YOUR HEARTS BE TROUBLED *and do not be afraid.*
JOHN 14:27

DATE _____

P – PRAISE

R – REPENT

A – ASK

Y – YIELD

E – ENTER

R – RESPOND

MY CONVERSATIONS WITH GOD

But the plans OF THE LORDS
STAND FIRM FOREVER, THE PURPOSES OF
HIS HEART THROUGH all generations.
PSALM 33:11

DATE _____

P – PRAISE

R – REPENT

A – ASK

Y – YIELD

E – ENTER

R – RESPOND

MY CONVERSATIONS WITH GOD

P – PRAISE

R – REPENT

A – ASK

Y – YIELD

E – ENTER

R – RESPOND

If you BELONG TO CHRIST,
THEN YOU ARE ABRAHAM'S SEED, AND
HEIRS ACCORDING *to the promise.*
GALATIANS 3:29

DATE _____

P – PRAISE

_____

_____

R – REPENT

_____

_____

A – ASK

_____

_____

Y – YIELD

_____

_____

E – ENTER

_____

_____

R – RESPOND

_____

_____

MY CONVERSATIONS WITH GOD

THE LORD IS COMPASSIONATE
AND GRACIOUS, SLOW TO ANGER,
abounding in love.
PSALM 103:8

P – PRAISE

R – REPENT

A – ASK

Y – YIELD

E – ENTER

R – RESPOND

I WILL GIVE YOU A *new heart* AND PUT A
NEW SPIRIT IN YOU; I WILL REMOVE FROM YOU YOUR
heart of stone AND GIVE YOU A *heart of flesh.*
EZEKIEL 36:26

DATE _____

P – PRAISE

R – REPENT

A – ASK

Y – YIELD

E – ENTER

R – RESPOND

MY CONVERSATIONS WITH GOD

FOR IT IS GOD WHO WORKS
IN YOU TO WILL AND TO *act in order*
to fulfill HIS GOOD PURPOSE.
PHILIPPIANS 2:13

_____

_____

_____

_____

_____

_____

_____

_____

_____

_____

_____

_____

_____

_____

_____

_____

_____

_____

DATE _____

P – PRAISE

R – REPENT

A – ASK

Y – YIELD

E – ENTER

R – RESPOND

MY CONVERSATIONS WITH GOD

The Lord bless you AND KEEP YOU; THE LORD
MAKE HIS face shine ON YOU AND BE GRACIOUS TO YOU;
THE LORD TURN HIS FACE TOWARD YOU AND give you peace.

NUMBERS 6:24-26

DATE _____

P – PRAISE
_____
_____

R – REPENT
_____
_____

A – ASK
_____
_____

Y – YIELD
_____
_____

E – ENTER
_____
_____

R – RESPOND
_____
_____
_____

MY CONVERSATIONS WITH GOD

YOU WILL SEEK ME AND
find me when YOU SEEK ME
WITH ALL *your heart.*
JEREMIAH 29:13

DATE _____

P – PRAISE

R – REPENT

A – ASK

Y – YIELD

E – ENTER

R – RESPOND

MY CONVERSATIONS WITH GOD

IN ALL THESE THINGS WE
are more than conquerors
THROUGH HIM WHO LOVED US.
ROMANS 8:37

DATE _____

P – PRAISE

R – REPENT

A – ASK

Y – YIELD

E – ENTER

R – RESPOND

MY CONVERSATIONS WITH GOD

DATE _____

P – PRAISE

R – REPENT

A – ASK

Y – YIELD

E – ENTER

R – RESPOND

BUT NOW, HE HAS RECONCILED YOU *by Christ's* PHYSICAL BODY THROUGH DEATH TO PRESENT YOU HOLY IN *his sight,* WITHOUT BLEMISH AND *free from accusation.*

COLOSSIANS 1:22

DATE _____

P – PRAISE

R – REPENT

A – ASK

Y – YIELD

E – ENTER

R – RESPOND

MY CONVERSATIONS WITH GOD

As for God, HIS WAY IS PERFECT:
THE LORD'S WORD IS FLAWLESS;
he shields ALL WHO TAKE REFUGE IN HIM.

2 SAMUEL 22:31

DATE _____

P – PRAISE
_____
_____

R – REPENT
_____
_____

A – ASK
_____
_____

Y – YIELD
_____
_____

E – ENTER
_____
_____

R – RESPOND
_____
_____

MY CONVERSATIONS WITH GOD

BUT OUR CITIZENSHIP IS IN HEAVEN.
and we eagerly AWAIT A SAVIOR FROM
THERE, *the Lord Jesus Christ.*
PHILIPPIANS 3:20

DATE _____

P – PRAISE
_____
_____

R – REPENT
_____
_____

A – ASK
_____
_____

Y – YIELD
_____
_____

E – ENTER
_____
_____

R – RESPOND
_____
_____

MY CONVERSATIONS WITH GOD

NOW FAITH IS CONFIDENCE IN
what we hope for AND ASSURANCE
ABOUT WHAT *we do not see.*
HEBREWS 11:1

DATE _____

P – PRAISE

_____

_____

R – REPENT

_____

_____

A – ASK

_____

_____

Y – YIELD

_____

_____

E – ENTER

_____

_____

R – RESPOND

_____

_____

MY CONVERSATIONS WITH GOD

THE FRUIT OF THE SPIRIT *is love, joy, peace*, FORBEARANCE, KINDNESS, GOODNESS, FAITHFULNESS, GENTLENESS AND SELF-CONTROL. *Against such things* THERE IS NO LAW.

GALATIANS 5:22-23

DATE _____

P – PRAISE

_____

_____

R – REPENT

_____

_____

A – ASK

_____

_____

Y – YIELD

_____

_____

E – ENTER

_____

_____

R – RESPOND

_____

_____

MY CONVERSATIONS WITH GOD

Charm is deceptive, AND BEAUTY IS
FLEETING; BUT A WOMAN WHO FEARS
THE LORD, *is to be praised.*
PROVERBS 31:30

_____

_____

_____

_____

_____

_____

_____

_____

_____

_____

_____

_____

_____

_____

_____

_____

_____

_____

_____

_____

MY
Conversations
WITH God

ABOUT MICHELLE PRINCE

Michelle Prince is a best-selling author, sought-after motivational speaker, self-publishing expert, life coach, and CEO/Founder of Performance Publishing Group, a partner publishing company dedicated to making a difference ... one story at a time. Michelle knows we all have a story, and she is passionate about helping others to share their story for God's glory.

Through her books, courses, speaking and seminars, Michelle helps people to ignite their passion, identify their God-given purpose, achieve balance, overcome procrastination, unlock potential, and be more productive to achieve abundant success in their personal and professional lives.

To learn more, go to MichellePrince.com.

Looking for a truly unique and memorable gift? Give your loved ones the gift of journaling so that they can experience God's love in a more personal way.

MyConversationsWithGod.org

www.ingramcontent.com/pod-product-compliance
Lightning Source LLC
Chambersburg PA
CBHW061408090426
42740CB00024B/3475